Let's Get Cooking

SUPER JUICING

Over **100** nutritious drinks

igloobooks

igloobooks

Published in 2017
by Igloo Books Ltd
Cottage Farm
Sywell
NN6 0BJ
www.igloobooks.com

Designed by Nicholas Gage
Edited by Bobby Newlyn-Jones

Food photography and recipe development
© Stockfood, The Food Media Agency
Additional imagery © iStock / Getty Images
Cover images: © iStock / Getty Images

LEO002 0417
2 4 6 8 10 9 7 5 3 1
ISBN 978-1-78557-486-3

Printed and manufactured in China

Contents

Fruity Drinks

SERVES: **4** | PREPARATION TIME: **4 MINS**

Strawberry and Bilberry Juice

300 g / 10 ½ oz / 2 cups strawberries, hulled

150 g / 5 oz / 1 cup seedless red grapes

150 g / 5 oz / 1 cup bilberries (use blueberries if not available)

a few drops of vanilla extract

250 g / 9 oz / 1 cup crushed ice

1. Combine the strawberries, grapes, bilberries, vanilla extract and crushed ice in a blender.
2. Blitz until smooth before pouring into glasses.
3. Serve immediately or cover and chill for up to 1 hour.

SERVES: **4** | PREPARATION TIME: **5 MINS**

Melon and Kiwi Smoothie

6 kiwi fruit, peeled and chopped
1 small Galia melon, deseeded and flesh chopped
½ lemon, juiced
a few drops of vanilla extract
250 g / 9 oz / 1 cup crushed ice

1. Combine the kiwi fruit, melon, lemon juice in a blender.
2. Add the vanilla extract.
3. Blitz until smooth before adding the crushed ice and blitzing again.
4. Pour into glasses and serve immediately for best results.

Pineapple Smoothie

1 medium pineapple, peeled and cored
250 g / 9 oz / 1 2/3 cups strawberries,
   hulled
2 medium bananas, chopped
150 g / 5 oz / 2/3 cup strawberry yogurt
250 g / 9 oz / 1 cup crushed ice

1. Chop the pineapple flesh and combine it with the strawberries, banana and yogurt in a blender.
2. Blitz until smooth before adding the crushed ice; blitz again.
3. Pour into glasses and serve immediately.

Orange and Papaya Juice

4 oranges, segmented
2 ripe papayas, deseeded and
   flesh chopped
1 lemon, juiced
250 g / 9 oz / 1 cup crushed ice
a small handful of mint leaves,
   to garnish

1. Blitz together the orange segments, papaya flesh and lemon juice in a blender.
2. Pass the juice through a sieve and back into the blender.
3. Add the crushed ice and blitz again until smooth.
4. Pour into glasses and garnish with mint leaves on top.
5. Serve immediately for best results.

Peach, Orange and Lemon Juice

4 ripe peaches, pitted and chopped
4 oranges, juiced
2 lemons, juiced
1 tbsp agave nectar
a few drops of vanilla extract
250 g / 9 oz / 1 cup crushed ice
a few sprigs of red basil, to garnish

1. Combine the peach, orange juice, lemon juice, agave nectar, vanilla extract and crushed ice in a blender.
2. Blitz until smooth; pass through a fine sieve into a jug.
3. Cover and chill for up to 1 hour.
4. Pour the juice in glasses and garnish with red basil before serving.

Apricot Smoothie

1 medium pineapple, peeled
  and cored
4 ripe apricots, pitted
1 lime, juiced
250 g / 9 oz / 1 cup crushed ice

1. Chop the pineapple flesh and
   apricots before adding to a blender
   with the lime juice.
2. Blitz until smooth before adding
   the crushed ice and blitzing again
   until smooth.
3. Pass the smoothie through a sieve
   into a jug before pouring into
   glasses and serving.

Grapefruit Smoothie

2 pink grapefruit, segmented
2 medium bananas, chopped
1 large ripe mango, pitted and
  flesh chopped
1 lime, juiced
150 g / 5 oz / 2/3 cup plain yogurt
250 g / 9 oz / 1 cup crushed ice

1. Combine the pink grapefruit, banana, mango, lime juice and yogurt in a blender.
2. Blitz until smooth before adding the crushed ice; blitz again.
3. Pour into glasses and serve immediately.

Lime and Raspberry Juice

6 limes
300 g / 10 ½ oz / 2 cups raspberries
1 l / 1 pint 16 fl. oz / 4 cups cold water
2 tbsp agave nectar
250 g / 9 oz / 1 cup ice cubes

1. Halve four of the limes and juice into a jug.
2. Add the raspberries, water and agave nectar; churn with a bar spoon for 30 seconds before covering and chilling for 1 hour.
3. After 1 hour, slice the remaining limes thinly and add to the jug with the ice cubes.
4. Stir briefly before serving.

Papaya Smoothie

1 small pineapple, peeled and cored
1 ripe papaya, deseeded and
  flesh chopped
1 large ripe mango, pitted and
  flesh chopped
1 lime, juiced
110 g / 4 oz / ½ cup plain yogurt
250 g / 9 oz / 1 cup crushed ice

1. Chop the pineapple flesh before adding to a blender along with the papaya, mango, lime juice and yogurt.
2. Blitz until smooth before adding the crushed ice; blitz again.
3. Pour into glasses and serve immediately.

Grape Smoothie

2 large gala apples, cored and chopped
200 g / 7 oz / 1 1/3 cups white
  seedless grapes
200 g / 7 oz / 1 1/3 cups red
  seedless grapes
250 g / 9 oz / 1 cup crushed ice

1. Pass the apples and grapes through a juicer; collect the juice.
2. Combine the juice and crushed ice in a blender and blitz until smooth.
3. Pass through a sieve into glasses before serving.

SERVES: **4** | PREPARATION TIME: **10 MINS**

Orange and Banana Juice

2 large ripe bananas, chopped
4 oranges, segmented
1 tbsp honey
250 g / 9 oz / 1 cup crushed ice

1. Blitz together the chopped bananas, orange segments, honey and crushed ice in a blender until smooth.
2. Pour through a sieve into a jug before pouring into glasses.
3. Serve immediately for best results.

Peach Smoothie

2 ripe peaches, pitted and chopped
2 Braeburn apples, cored and chopped
300 g / 10 ½ oz / 2 cups raspberries
110 g / 4 oz / ½ cup raspberry yogurt
250 g / 9 oz / 1 cup crushed ice

1. Pass the peach and apple through a juicer; collect the juice.
2. Combine the juice with the raspberries, raspberry yogurt and crushed ice in a blender; blitz until smooth.
3. Pour into glasses and serve immediately.

SERVES: **4** | PREPARATION TIME: **5 MINS**

Apple and
Pear Smoothie

2 Granny Smith apples, cored
  and chopped
2 Rocha pears, cored and chopped
1 head of iceberg lettuce, shredded
250 ml / 9 fl. oz / 1 cup skimmed milk
125 g / 4 ½ oz / ½ cup ice cubes

1. Blitz together the apple, pear,
   lettuce and milk in a food processor
   until smooth.
2. Add the ice cubes and blitz again
   until the smoothie is chilled.
3. Pass the liquid through a sieve into
   a jug; cover and chill until ready
   to serve.

Pear Smoothie

3 Conference pears, cored
  and chopped
½ head of white cabbage, shredded
4 sticks of celery, peeled and chopped
250 ml / 9 fl. oz / 1 cup fresh
  apple juice
125 g / 4 ½ oz / ½ cup crushed iced

1. Pass the pears, cabbage and celery through a juicer; collect the juice.
2. Combine the pressed juice with the apple juice and crushed ice in a blender.
3. Blitz until smooth; pass through a sieve into a jug.
4. Cover and chill until ready to serve.

Mandarin Smoothie

2 Comice pears, cored and chopped
4 mandarins, peeled and segmented
4 apricots, pitted and chopped
125 ml / 4 ½ fl. oz / ½ cup fresh
   orange juice
250 g / 9 oz / 1 cup crushed ice

1. Combine the pear, mandarin segments, apricot, orange juice and crushed ice in a blender.
2. Blitz until smooth before passing through a fine sieve into a jug.
3. Pour into short glasses and serve immediately.

Strawberry Smoothie

2 Conference pears, cored
   and chopped
300 g / 10 ½ oz / 2 cups strawberries,
   hulled and chopped
225 g / 8 oz / 1 ½ cups black
   cherries, pitted
250 g / 9 oz / 1 cup crushed ice

1. Combine the pears, strawberries and cherries in a blender; blitz until smooth.
2. Add the crushed ice and blitz again before pouring into glasses.
3. Serve immediately for best results.

SERVES: **4** | PREPARATION TIME: **5 MINS**

Summer Fruit Smoothie

150 g / 5 oz / 1 cup strawberries, hulled and chopped
150 g / 5 oz / 1 cup blackberries
150 g / 5 oz / 1 cup raspberries
110 g / 4 oz / 1 cup redcurrants
350 g / 12 oz / 1 ½ cups crushed iced
a drop of vanilla extract

1. Combine all the ingredients in a blender; blitz until slushy.
2. Pour into glasses and serve immediately for best results.
3. Alternatively, you can cover and chill the smoothie for up to 2 hours before
   serving for a thinner consistency.

Watermelon and Strawberry Smoothie

½ watermelon, peeled and cut
  into chunks
300 g / 10 ½ oz / 2 cups strawberries,
  hulled and chopped
1 lime, juiced
110 g / 4 oz / ½ cup plain yogurt
250 g / 9 oz / 1 cup crushed ice
a few sprigs of basil, chopped

1. Combine the watermelon, strawberries, lime juice and yogurt in a blender.
2. Blitz until smooth; add the crushed ice and blitz again briefly until the ice has mostly dissolved.
3. Pour into glasses and top with a sprinkle of basil before serving.

Orange, Mint and Tomato Smoothie

225 g / 8 oz / 1 ½ cups cherry
  tomatoes, halved
6 medium oranges, peeled
  and segmented
a small bunch of mint, roughly chopped
250 g / 9 oz / 1 cup crushed ice
a pinch of salt
extra sprigs of mint, to garnish

1. Combine the cherry tomato halves, orange segments, chopped mint, crushed ice and a pinch of salt in a blender.
2. Blitz until smooth; pass through a sieve into a jug.
3. Pour into glasses and garnish with mint sprigs before serving.

SERVES: **4** | PREPARATION TIME: **5-10 MINS**

Peach and Raspberry Smoothie

2 ripe peaches, pitted and chopped
300 g / 10 ½ oz / 2 cups raspberries
2 Cox or Gala apples, cored and sliced
1 lime, juiced
1 lemon, juiced
250 g / 9 oz / 1 cup crushed ice

1. Pass the peach, raspberries and apple through a juicer; collect the juice.
2. Combine the juice with the lime and lemon juices in a blender.
3. Stir well and add the crushed ice; blitz until smooth.
4. Pour into glasses and serve immediately.

SERVES: **4** | PREPARATION TIME: **5-10 MINS**

Watermelon and Bilberry Smoothie

½ watermelon, peeled and cut into chunks
225 g / 8 oz / 1 ½ cups bilberries (use blueberries if not available)
2 large cucumbers, roughly chopped
150 g / 5 oz / ⅔ cup crushed ice

1. Blitz together the watermelon, bilberries and cucumber in a blender.
2. Pass through a sieve back into the blender before adding the crushed ice.
3. Blitz again until chilled; cover and chill before serving.

Pomegranate, Kiwi and Lime Smoothie

6 kiwi fruit, peeled and chopped
1 pomegranate, halved and deseeded
2 limes, juiced
110 g / 4 oz / ½ cup plain yogurt
250 g / 9 oz / 1 cup crushed ice

1. Combine the kiwi fruit, most of the pomegranate seeds, lime juice, yogurt and crushed ice in a blender.
2. Blitz until smooth; pour into glasses.
3. Top with the remaining pomegranate seeds before serving.

Blueberry Juice with Frozen Banana

2 bananas, peeled and sliced
300 g / 10 ½ oz / 2 cups blueberries
1 apple, quartered

1. Spread the bananas out on a greaseproof paper lined baking tray and freeze for at least 2 hours or until solid. Transfer to a freezer bag and freeze until ready to use.
2. Process the blueberries and apple through an electronic juicer, according to the manufacturer's instructions.
3. Transfer the juice to a liquidizer and add the frozen banana.
4. Blend until smooth, then pour into a glass and serve immediately.

Passion Fruit and Papaya Smoothie

3 passion fruit, halved
1 papaya, deseeded with flesh chopped
2 golden delicious apples, cored and chopped
125 ml / 4 ½ fl. oz / ½ cup fresh orange juice
1 lime, juiced
250 g / 9 oz / 1 cup crushed ice

1. Add the passion fruit, papaya, apple, orange and lime juices; blitz until smooth before passing through a sieve back into the blender.
2. Add the crushed ice and blitz again until smooth.
3. Pour into glasses and serve immediately.

Peach, Avocado and Kiwi Smoothie

2 kiwi fruit, peeled and chopped
4 ripe peaches, pitted and chopped
1 small ripe avocado, pitted and chopped
1 lime, juiced
75 ml / 3 fl. oz / 1/3 cup skimmed milk
110 g / 4 oz / ½ cup plain low-fat yogurt
125 g / 4 ½ oz / ½ cup crushed ice

1. Combine the kiwi fruit, peach, avocado, lime juice, milk and yogurt in a blender; blitz until smooth.
2. Add the crushed ice and blitz again until combined.
3. Pour the smoothie into four small glasses and serve immediately.

SERVES: **8** | PREPARATION TIME: **10 MINS** | COOKING TIME: **8-10 MINS**

Goji Berry and Lime Smoothie

250 g / 9 oz / 2 cups cranberries
2 tbsp dried Goji berries
1 lime, juiced
250 ml / 9 fl. oz / 1 cup cold water
110 g / 4 oz / ½ cup plain yogurt
250 g / 9 oz / 1 cup crushed ice

1. Combine the cranberries, goji berries, lime juice and water in a small saucepan.
2. Cook over a medium heat, covered, for 8–10 minutes until the cranberries are completely soft and starting to burst.
3. Remove from the heat and leave to cool for 5 minutes before blitzing with the yogurt and crushed ice in a blender.
4. Pour into tall shot glasses and serve immediately.

Blueberry Smoothie

300 g / 10 ½ oz / 2 cups strawberries,
  hulled and chopped
200 g / 7 oz / 2 cups blueberries
250 ml / 9 fl. oz / 1 cup skimmed milk
250 g / 9 oz / 1 cup low-fat
  strawberry yogurt

1. Combine all the ingredients in a blender and blitz until smooth.
2. Stir well before pouring into a jug; cover and chill until ready to serve.
3. This smoothie is best served as soon after making as possible.

Apple, Berry and Grapefruit Juice

3 pink grapefruit, segmented with
  pith removed
2 Granny Smith apples, cored
  and chopped
75 g / 3 oz / ½ cup bilberries (use
  blueberries if not available)
2 sticks of celery, peeled and chopped
250 g / 9 oz / 1 cup crushed ice

1. Pass the pink grapefruit flesh, apple, bilberries and celery through a juicer;
   collect the juice.
2. Combine the juice and crushed ice in a blender and blitz until smooth.
3. Pass through a fine sieve into a jug.
4. Cover and chill or serve immediately for best results.

SERVES: **2** | PREPARATION TIME: **10 MINS** | FREEZING TIME: **3 HOURS**

Summer Berry Smoothie

450 g / 1 lb / 3 cups mixed summer berries
½ cantaloupe melon, peeled and cut into chunks
1 cucumber, cut into chunks
handful cranberries

1. Spread the berries out on a baking tray and freeze for 3 hours or until solid.
2. Process the cantaloupe and cucumber through an electronic juicer, according to the manufacturer's instructions.
3. Transfer the juice to a liquidizer and add the frozen berries. Blend until smooth, then pour into glasses.
4. Sprinkle with cranberries then serve.

Watermelon Refresher

450 g / 1 lb / 3 cups watermelon,
  peeled and diced
150 g / 5 ½ oz / 1 cup raspberries
6 mint leaves, plus a few more
  to garnish
2 apples, cut into chunks

1. Process the ingredients in the order shown through an electronic juicer,
   according to the manufacturer's instructions.
2. Serve the juice garnished with mint leaves.

Blackcurrant and Apple Smoothie

2 apples, cut into chunks
1 fennel bulb, cut into chunks
75 g / 2 ½ oz / ½ cup blackcurrants
2 ripe avocados, peeled and stoned
2 tsp agave nectar
mint leaves to garnish

1. Process the apple and fennel through an electronic juicer, according to the
   manufacturer's instructions.
2. Transfer the juice to a liquidizer and add the blackcurrants, avocado and
   agave nectar.
3. Blend until smooth, adding a handful of ice cubes to chill if preferred.
   Pour into glasses and serve immediately, garnished with mint.

SERVES: **2** | PREPARATION TIME: **10 MINS**

Blueberry and Orange Smoothie

3 medium beetroot, cut into chunks
2 oranges, peeled
100 g / 3 ½ oz / ⅔ cup blueberries,
  plus extra to garnish
1 large ripe banana, peeled
mint leaves to garnish

1. Process the beetroot and orange through an electronic juicer, according to the manufacturer's instructions.
2. Transfer the juice to a liquidizer and add the blackberries and the banana.
3. Blend until smooth, adding a handful of ice cubes to chill if preferred. Pour into glasses and serve immediately, garnished with blueberries and mint leaves.

SERVES: **4** | PREPARATION TIME: **10 MINS**

Peach and Apricot Smoothie

6 medium carrots, peeled
extra carrots, to garnish
3 large peaches, pitted and chopped
4 ripe apricots, pitted and halved
250 g / 9 oz / 1 cup crushed ice
1 lemon, juiced
a handful of mint

1. Pass the carrots, peaches and apricots through a juice; collect the juice.
2. Combine the juice with the crushed ice and lemon juice in a blender.
3. Blitz until smooth before pouring into glasses and garnish with a couple of mint leaves.

Strawberry Dream

400 g / 14 oz / 3 cups parsnip, sliced
½ honeydew melon, peeled and cut into chunks
150 g / 5 ½ oz / 1 cup strawberries
1 ripe banana, peeled

1. Process the parsnip and melon through an electronic juicer, according to the manufacturer's instructions.
2. Transfer the juice to a liquidizer and add the strawberries and banana.
3. Blend until smooth, adding a handful of ice cubes to chill if preferred. Pour into glasses and serve immediately.

Tropical Temptation

2 ripe mangoes, stoned and cut into chunks
1 pineapple, peeled and cut into chunks

1. Process the mangoes through an electronic juicer followed by the pineapple, according to the manufacturer's instructions.
2. Stir vigorously with a spoon to mix, then pour into glasses and serve immediately.

Blueberry Yogurt Smoothie

2 apples, quartered
250 g / 9 oz / 1 ⅔ cups blueberries
250 ml / 9 fl. oz / 1 cup thick
   Greek yogurt
2 sprigs lemon balm

1. Process the apples through an electronic juicer, according to the manufacturer's instructions.
2. Reserve a few blueberries for the garnish and put the rest in a liquidizer with the apple juice and yogurt. Blend until completely smooth, then pour into two glasses.
3. Garnish the smoothies with the reserved blueberries and sprigs of lemon balm.

Strawberry Linseed Shake

2 ripe bananas, peeled and sliced
150 g / 5 ½ oz / 1 cup strawberries,
  hulled
2 papaya, cut into chunks and
  seeds removed
3 pink grapefruit, peeled
1 tbsp golden linseeds, plus an extra
  sprinkle to garnish
mint to garnish

1. Spread the banana and strawberries out on a baking tray and freeze for
   3 hours or until solid.
2. Process the papaya and grapefruit through an electronic juicer, according
   to the manufacturer's instructions.
3. Transfer the juice to a liquidizer and add the linseeds and frozen fruit.
   Blend until smooth, then pour into a glass and garnish with mint and an
   extra sprinkle of linseeds.

Kiwi and Banana Blitz

8 kiwi fruit
2 ripe bananas, peeled and sliced

1. Process the kiwi fruit through an electronic juicer, according to the
   manufacturer's instructions.
2. Transfer the juice to a liquidizer and add the banana.
3. Blend until smooth, adding a handful of ice cubes to chill if preferred.
   Serve immediately.

SERVES: **4** | PREPARATION TIME: **5-10 MINS**

Apple and Carrot Juice

2 medium carrots, peeled and cut into large pieces
150 g / 5 oz / 1 cup cooked beetroot, cubed
2 Granny Smith apples, cored and chopped
1 orange, juiced
250 g / 9 oz / 1 cup crushed ice

1. Pass the carrots, beetroot and chopped apple through a juicer; collect
   the juice.
2. Combine the pressed juice with the orange juice and crushed ice in a blender.
3. Blitz until smooth before passing through a fine sieve into a jug.
4. Cover and chill until ready to serve in short glasses.

Vegetable Drinks

Beetroot and Broccoli Juice

1 small head of broccoli, prepared into
   small florets
4 small cooked beetroots, chopped
a pinch of salt
150 ml / 5 fl. oz / ⅔ cup cold water
110 g / 4 oz / ½ cup crushed ice

1. Bring a saucepan of water to a simmer; place the broccoli in a steaming basket and sit atop the saucepan.
2. Steam for 3–4 minutes until just tender. Remove and add to a blender with the beetroots, salt, water and crushed ice.
3. Blitz until smooth before passing through a sieve into a jug.
4. Pour into glasses and serve immediately.

Avocado Smoothie

100 g / 3 ½ oz / 2 cups watercress
1 medium ripe avocado, pitted and
   flesh chopped
1 large cucumber, chopped
150 ml / 5 fl. oz / ⅔ cup soy or
   almond milk
a pinch of salt
250 g / 9 oz / 1 cup crushed ice

1. Combine the watercress, avocado, cucumber and milk in a blender; blitz until completely smooth.
2. Add the crushed ice and salt and blitz again until smooth.
3. Pour into glasses and serve immediately.

SERVES: **4** | PREPARATION TIME: **10 MINS**

Carrot and Cabbage Juice

6 medium carrots, peeled
1 large Hispi cabbage, shredded
1 orange, juiced
150 ml / 5 fl. oz / ⅔ cup cold water
150 g / 5 oz / 2/3 cup crushed ice

1. Pass the carrots and cabbage through a juicer; collect the juice.
2. Add the juice to a blender with the orange juice, water and crushed ice.
3. Blitz until smooth before passing through a fine sieve into glasses.
4. Serve immediately or cover and chill for up to 1 hour.

SERVES: **4** | PREPARATION TIME: **10 MINS**

Super-green Juice

6 sticks of celery, peeled
1 large cucumber, sliced
1 large head of iceberg lettuce, shredded
1 lime, juiced
a pinch of salt
250 g / 9 oz / 1 cup crushed ice

1. Pass the celery, cucumber and lettuce through a juicer; collect the juice.
2. Combine the juice with the lime juice, salt and crushed ice in a blender.
3. Blitz until smooth before passing through a sieve into glasses.
4. Serve immediately.

SERVES: **4** | PREPARATION TIME: **10 MINS**

Carrot, Spinach and Celery Smoothie

6 medium carrots, peeled
4 sticks of celery, peeled
55 g / 2 oz / 1 cup baby spinach leaves, washed
110 g / 4 oz / ½ cup plain yogurt
250 g / 9 oz / 1 cup crushed ice.

1. Pass the carrots and celery sticks through a juicer; collect the juice.
2. Combine the juice with the spinach leaves, yogurt and ice in a blender.
3. Blitz until smooth before pouring into glasses.
4. Serve immediately for best results.

SERVES: 4 | PREPARATION TIME: 2 HOURS 10 MINS

Gazpacho

300 g / 10 ½ oz / 2 cups vine
  tomatoes, cored and chopped
1 large cucumber, chopped
4 sticks of celery, peeled
2 red peppers, chopped
1 green pepper, chopped
a pinch of salt and pepper
1 lime, juiced
250 g / 9 oz / 1 cup crushed ice

1. Pass the tomatoes, cucumber,
   celery and peppers through a
   juicer; collect the juice.
2. Combine the juice with a pinch of
   seasoning, lime juice and the
   crushed ice in a blender.
3. Blitz until smooth before straining
   into a jug.
4. Cover and chill for 2 hours before
   serving.

SERVES: **4** | PREPARATION TIME: **4 MINS** | CHILLING TIME: **3 HOURS**

Tomato Cocktail

300 g / 10 ½ oz / 2 cups cherry tomatoes, halved
1 large cucumber, thinly sliced
1 l / 1 pint 16 fl. oz / 4 cups cold water
½ lime, juiced
a pinch of salt
350 g / 12 oz / 1 ½ cups ice cubes

1. Mix together the tomatoes, cucumber slices, water, lime juice and the salt in a jug.
2. Churn with a bar spoon for 30 seconds; cover and chill for 3 hours.
3. After chilling, pour into ice-filled glasses and serve.

Broccoli Smoothie

2 small heads of broccoli, prepared
into small florets
2 Granny Smith apples, cored
and chopped
150 g / 5 oz / 3 cups baby spinach
110 g / 4 oz / ½ cup plain yogurt
1 tsp wheatgrass powder
250 g / 9 oz / 1 cup crushed ice

1. Pass the broccoli and apple
   through a juicer; collect the juice.
2. Combine the juice with the spinach,
   yogurt, wheatgrass powder and
   crushed ice in a blender.
3. Blitz until smooth before pouring
   into glasses.
4. Serve immediately for best results.

Cucumber Smoothie

1 large cucumber, sliced
4 carrots, peeled
1 large ripe avocado, pitted and
  flesh chopped
1 orange, juiced
110 ml / 4 fl. oz / ½ cup almond milk
250 g / 9 oz / 1 cup crushed ice

1. Pass the cucumber and carrots through a juicer; collect the juice.
2. Combine the juice with the avocado, orange juice, almond milk and crushed ice in a blender.
3. Blitz until smooth before pouring into short glasses and serving.

Red Pepper and Ginger Smoothie

2 red peppers, chopped
5 cm (2 in) piece of root ginger, peeled
4 medium carrots, peeled
a pinch of cayenne pepper
110 g / 4 oz / ½ cup plain yogurt
250 g / 9 oz / 1 cup crushed ice

1. Pass the peppers, ginger and carrots through a juicer; collect the juice.
2. Combine the juice with the cayenne pepper, yogurt and crushed ice in a blender; blitz until smooth.
3. Pour into glasses and serve immediately for best results.

Cucumber and Kiwi Smoothie

2 large cucumbers, chopped
2 kiwi fruit, peeled and diced
250 g / 9 oz / 1 cup plain low-fat yogurt
250 g / 9 oz / 1 cup crushed ice
a pinch of salt

1. Combine the cucumber and kiwi fruit in a blender; blitz until slushy.
2. Add the yogurt and ice and blitz again until liquid and smooth.
3. Pour into glasses and serve immediately for best results.

Fennel and Asparagus Smoothie

250 g / 9 oz / 1 ⅔ cups asparagus
  spears, woody ends removed
1 large cucumber
1 bulb of fennel, thinly sliced
1 lime, juiced
150 ml / 5 fl. oz / ⅔ cup cold water
175 g / 6 oz / ¾ cup crushed ice

1. Place a steaming basket over a saucepan of simmering water; add the asparagus to the basket and steam for 3–4 minutes until just tender.
2. Chop and add to a blender with the cucumber, fennel, lime juice, water and crushed ice.
3. Blitz until smooth before passing through a sieve into a jug.
4. Pour into glasses and serve immediately.

SERVES: **4** | PREPARATION TIME: **10 MINS**

Lettuce and Tomato Juice

400 g / 14 oz / 2 ⅔ cups cherry tomatoes, halved
2 heads of Romaine lettuce, chopped
2 cucumbers, peeled and chopped
a pinch of salt
325 g / 11 oz / 1 ⅓ cups crushed ice

1. Pass the cherry tomatoes, lettuce and cucumber through a juicer; collect the juice.
2. Add the juice and a pinch of salt to a blender along with the crushed ice.
3. Blitz until smooth before pouring into glasses and serving.

Radish and Strawberry Juice

175 g / 6 oz / 1 ½ cups radishes
125 g / 4 ½ oz / ¾ cup strawberries, halved if large
1 large handful radish shoots, plus extra to garnish
150 g / 5 ½ oz / 1 ¼ cup parsnip, cubed
125 ml / 4 ½ fl. oz / ½ cup milk (optional)

1. Process the vegetables and fruit through an electronic juicer in the order shown, according to the manufacturer's instructions.
2. Pour the juice into a glass and make into a longer drink with milk, if preferred.
3. Serve garnished with radish shoots.

SERVES: **2** | PREPARATION TIME: **5 MINS**

Pumpkin and Cantaloupe Juice

600 g / 1 lb 5 oz / 5 cups pumpkin, peeled, seeded and sliced

1 cantaloupe melon, peeled, seeded and sliced

1. Process the ingredients through an electronic juicer, according to the manufacturer's instructions.
2. Pour the juice into two glasses and serve immediately.

SERVES: **2** | PREPARATION TIME: **10 MINS** | COOKING TIME: **15 MINS**

Sweet Potato and Carrot Smoothie

3 sweet potatoes, halved and sliced
4 carrots
1 onion, peeled and quartered
2 cloves of garlic, peeled
parsley, to garnish

1. Reserve one of the sweet potatoes and process the rest through an electronic juicer with the carrots, onion and garlic.
2. Dice the reserved sweet potato and put it in a saucepan with the juice and a pinch of salt. Cover with a lid and cook over a medium heat for 15 minutes or until the sweet potato is tender.
3. Blend until smooth in a liquidizer and serve hot or chilled, garnished with parsley.

Parsnip and Honeydew Juice

400 g / 14 oz / 3 cups parsnip, sliced
1 large wedge honeydew melon
175 g / 6 oz / 1 ¼ cups strawberries

1. Process all ingredients alternately through an electronic juicer, according to the manufacturer's instructions.
2. Pour the juice into a bottle and serve immediately with a straw.

Yellow Pepper and Kale Juice

3 yellow peppers
100 g / 3 ½ oz / 3 cups kale, chopped
200 g / 7 oz / 2 cups broccoli florets
1 bulb fennel, quartered
2 apples, quartered

1. Process all the ingredients through an electronic juicer, according to the manufacturer's instructions.
2. Stir well, then pour the juice into two glasses and serve immediately.

Super Juices

SERVES: **1** | PREPARATION TIME: **5 MINS**

Orange, Guava and Cantaloupe Juice

2 oranges, 1 slice reserved, the rest cut into wedges

3 guava, quartered

300 g / 10 ½ oz / 2 cups cantaloupe melon, seeds removed and diced

1. Process the ingredients through an electronic juicer, according to the manufacturer's instructions.

2. Pour the juice into a glass and serve immediately, garnished with the reserved orange slice.

Fruits of the Forest Juice

150 g / 5 ½ oz / 1 cup mixed berries
2 pears, quartered
100 g / 3 ½ oz / 1 cup red grapes
1 tsp chia seeds

1. Process the berries, pears and grapes through an electronic juicer, according to the manufacturer's instructions.
2. Pour into a glass and garnish with chia seeds.
3. To prevent the juice from separating, stir in the chia seeds and chill for around 10 minutes while the chia seeds swell and thicken the juice.

Watermelon and Pear Juice with Frozen Strawberries

375 g / 13 oz / 2 ½ cups watermelon, cut into chunks
2 pears, quartered
225 g / 8 oz / 1 ½ cups frozen strawberries

1. Process the watermelon and pears through an electronic juicer, according to the manufacturer's instructions.
2. Transfer the juice to a liquidizer and add the frozen strawberries.
3. Blend until smooth, then pour into a glass and serve immediately with a straw.

Hedgerow Juice

300 g / 10 ½ oz / 2 cups blackberries
2 pears, quartered
4 plums, halved and stoned
2 apples, quartered
mint sprigs, to garnish

1. Process the ingredients through an electronic juicer in the order shown, according to the manufacturer's instructions.
2. Store in a bottle in the fridge if not served straight away.
3. Pour into chilled glasses and serve garnished with mint.

SERVES: **2** | PREPARATION TIME: **15 MINS**

Green Juice with Chia and Goji Berries

2 cucumbers
100 g / 3 ½ oz / 3 cups watercress
2 medium apples, quartered
1 handful basil leaves
1 green pepper, quartered and
  seeds removed
50 g / 1 ¾ oz / ¼ cup chia seeds
1 tbsp goji berries

1. Process the cucumbers, watercress, apples, basil and green pepper through an electronic juicer in the order shown, according to the manufacturer's instructions.
2. Stir in the chia seeds, then chill for around 10 minutes to allow the seeds to swell and thicken the juice.
3. Stir well, then pour into two glasses and serve garnished with goji berries.

SERVES: **1** | PREPARATION TIME: **5 MINS**

Orange and Mango Juice

2 medium oranges, quartered
1 mango, stoned and sliced

1. Process the oranges and mango through an electronic juicer, according to the manufacturer's instructions.
2. Pour the juice into a glass and serve immediately with a straw.
3. This is delicious served with crushed ice mixed into the juice too.

SERVES: **4** | PREPARATION TIME: **10 MINS**

Tomato and Carrot Juice

300 g / 10 ½ oz / 2 cups cherry tomatoes on the vine, picked and chopped
4 medium carrots, peeled
4 sticks of celery, peeled
1 orange, juiced
250 g / 9 oz / 1 cup crushed ice

1. Pass the tomatoes, carrots and celery through a juicer; collect the juice.
2. Combine the juice with the orange juice and crushed ice in a blender.
3. Blitz until smooth before pouring into glasses and serving.

Celery and Carrot Juice

4 large carrots, peeled
4 sticks of celery, peeled
1 apple, cored and chopped
55 g / 2 oz / 1 cup baby spinach, washed
1 orange, juiced
250 g / 9 oz / 1 cup crushed ice

1. Pass the carrots, celery and apple through a juicer; collect the juice.
2. Add the juice to a blender with the spinach, orange juice and crushed ice; blitz until smooth.
3. Pass the juice through a fine sieve into a jug.
4. Pour into glasses and serve immediately for best results.

Watermelon Refresher with Frozen Berries

375 g / 13 oz / 2 ½ cups watermelon,
  cut into chunks
225 g / 8 oz / 1 ½ cups frozen mixed
  berries, plus extra to garnish
lemon balm, to garnish

1. Process the watermelon through an electronic juicer, according to the manufacturer's instructions.
2. Transfer the juice to a liquidizer and add the frozen berries.
3. Blend until smooth, then pour into a glass and garnish with berries and lemon balm.

Blueberry and Coconut Milkshake

350 g / 12 ½ oz / 2 cups pineapple,
  cut into chunks
350 g / 12 ½ oz / 2 ⅓ cups frozen
  blueberries
200 ml / 7 fl. oz / ¾ cup coconut milk
6 fresh blueberries, to garnish

1. Process the pineapple through an electronic juicer, according to the manufacturer's instructions.
2. Transfer the juice to a liquidizer with the frozen blueberries and the coconut milk.
3. Blend until smooth, then pour into two glasses.
4. Garnish each glass with three blueberries and serve with a straw.

SERVES: **4** | PREPARATION TIME: **10 MINS**

Turnip and Carrot Juice

6 medium carrots, peeled
2 turnips, peeled and chopped
75 g / 3 oz / 1 ½ cups baby
   spinach, washed
a pinch of salt
175 ml / 6 fl. oz / ¾ cup almond milk
250 g / 9 oz / 1 cup crushed ice

1. Pass the carrots and turnips through a juicer; collect the juice.
2. Combine the juice with the spinach, salt, almond milk and crushed ice in a blender.
3. Blitz until smooth before pouring into glasses and serving.

SERVES: **2** | PREPARATION TIME: **5 MINS** | CHILLING TIME: **2 HOURS**

Ginger, Lime and Mint Refresher

10 cm (4 in) piece of root ginger, peeled
2 limes, juiced
2 tbsp agave nectar
1 l / 1 pint 16 fl. oz / 4 cups cold water
a small bunch of mint leaves

1. Finely grate the ginger before mixing with the lime juice, agave nectar, cold water and most of the mint in a large jug.
2. Stir well, cover, and chill for 2 hours.
3. After 2 hours, strain the liquid through a fine sieve into glasses.
4. Garnish with the remaining mint before serving.

SERVES: **4** | PREPARATION TIME: **10 MINS**

Barley Juice

4 medium carrots, peeled
4 large Braeburn apples, cored and chopped
4 small cooked beetroots, chopped
a small handful of mint leaves
110 ml / 4 fl. oz / ½ cup aloe vera juice
2 tsp barley juice powder
½ tsp wheatgrass powder
250 g / 9 oz / 1 cup crushed ice

1. Pass the carrots, apples and beetroots through a juicer; collect the juice.
2. Combine the juice with the mint leaves, aloe vera juice, barley juice and wheatgrass powder in a blender.
3. Blitz until smooth before adding the crushed ice.
4. Blitz again before pouring into glasses; serve immediately for best results.

SERVES: **4** | PREPARATION TIME: **5 MINS**

Celery and Watermelon Juice

½ watermelon, peeled and cut
into chunks
4 sticks of celery, peeled and chopped
1 orange, juiced
½ lime, juiced
250 g / 9 oz / 1 cup crushed ice

1. Combine the watermelon, celery,
   orange and lime juices and crushed
   ice in a blender.
2. Blitz until smooth; pour into
   glasses and serve immediately for
   best results.

SERVES: **4** | PREPARATION TIME: **10 MINS**

Beetroot and Carrot Almond Milkshake

1 large globe artichoke, peeled
  and trimmed
1 lemon, juiced
3 small cooked beetroots, chopped
2 large carrots, peeled
3 sticks of celery, peeled
150 ml / 5 fl. oz / 2/3 cup almond milk
2 tsp wheatgrass powder
250 g / 9 oz / 1 cup crushed ice

1. Rub the artichoke with the lemon juice before passing through a juicer along with the beetroots, carrots and celery; collect the juice.
2. Combine the juice with the almond milk, wheatgrass powder and ice in a blender; blitz until smooth.
3. Pour into glasses and serve immediately for best results.

SERVES: **4** | PREPARATION TIME: **5 MINS**

Tomato and Grapefruit Smoothie

250 g / 9 oz / 1 ⅔ cups vine tomatoes, cored and chopped
4 pink grapefruit, segmented
1 Hispi cabbage, shredded
250 g / 9 oz / 1 cup plain yogurt
250 g / 9 oz / 1 cup crushed ice

1. Blitz together the tomatoes, pink grapefruit and cabbage in a blender until smooth.
2. Add the yogurt and crushed ice and blitz again before pouring into glasses.
3. Serve immediately for best results.

SERVES: **1** | PREPARATION TIME: **5 MINS**

Freshly Pressed Pomegranate Juice

2 large pomegranates, quartered

1. Process the pomegranates through an electronic juicer, according to the manufacturer's instructions.
2. Sieve the juice into a glass to ensure it is completely smooth.
3. Delicious served with summer berries.

SERVES: **4** | PREPARATION TIME: **10 MINS** | CHILLING TIME: **2 HOURS**

Cucumber, Coriander and Carrot Juice

2 large cucumbers, chopped
4 small carrots, peeled and chopped
a small bunch of coriander (cilantro), chopped
a pinch of salt and pepper
1 lime, juiced
250 g / 9 oz / 1 cup crushed ice

1. Pass the cucumbers and carrots through a juicer; collect the juice.
2. Combine the juice with the coriander, a pinch of seasoning, lime juice and the crushed ice in a blender.
3. Blitz until smooth before straining into a jug.
4. Cover and chill for 2 hours before serving.

SERVES: **2** | PREPARATION TIME: **5 MINS**

Orange, Cranberry and Grape Juice

3 oranges, quartered
400 g / 14 oz / 4 cups cranberries
150 g / 5 ½ oz / 1 cup red grapes

1. Slice one of the orange quarters and reserve for the garnish with a handful of cranberries.
2. Process the rest of the ingredients through an electronic juicer, according to the manufacturer's instructions.
3. Pour the juice into two glasses and add the orange slices. Thread the reserved cranberries onto a couple of cocktail sticks and add one to each glass.

SERVES: **4** | PREPARATION TIME: **10 MINS**

Carrot, Beetroot and Strawberry Drink

4 medium carrots, peeled
4 small cooked beetroot, chopped
300 g / 10 ½ oz / 2 cups strawberries, hulled
2 oranges, juiced
250 g / 9 oz / 1 cup crushed ice

1. Pass the carrots and beetroots through a juicer; collect the juice.
2. Combine the juice with the orange juice and crushed ice in a blender; blitz until smooth.
3. Pass the juice through a sieve into glasses and serve immediately.

Grapefruit, Guava and Papaya Juice

3 pink grapefruit, cut into wedges
1 handful ice cubes
3 guava, quartered
1 large papaya, seeds removed
  and sliced
mint sprig, to garnish

1. Slice one of the grapefruit wedges and put it in a glass with the ice.
2. Process the rest of the grapefruit through an electronic juicer with the guava and papaya, according to the manufacturer's instructions.
3. Pour the juice into a glass and serve immediately, garnished with mint.

Freshly Pressed Apple Juice

3 medium apples
1 cm (½ in) root ginger

1. Process the apples and root ginger through an electronic juicer, according to the manufacturer's instructions.
2. Sieve into a glass and serve as soon as possible.
3. Can be served with crushed ice.

SERVES: **4** | PREPARATION TIME: **10 MINS**

Pineapple and Celery Juice

1 small pineapple, peeled and cored
4 sticks of celery, peeled
2 small iceberg lettuce, shredded
55 ml / 2 fl. oz / ¼ cup aloe vera juice
1 lime, juiced
1 tbsp agave nectar
110 g / 4 oz / ½ cup plain yogurt
250 g / 9 oz / 1 cup crushed ice

1. Chop the pineapple flesh and pass through a juicer with the celery and lettuce; collect the juice.
2. Combine the juice with the aloe vera juice, lime juice, agave nectar, yogurt and crushed ice; blitz until smooth.
3. Pour into glasses and serve immediately for best results.

Grape, Celery and Pineapple Juice

8 sticks of celery, peeled and chopped
1 head of iceberg lettuce, shredded
1 small pineapple, peeled, cored and diced
300 g / 10 ½ oz / 2 cups white seedless grapes
250 g / 9 oz / 1 cup crushed ice

1. Pass the celery and lettuce through the juicer, collecting the juice.
2. Follow with the pineapple and grapes; pass the juice from the fruit through a sieve before combining with the celery and lettuce juice in a blender.
3. Add the crushed ice and blitz until smooth.
4. Pour into glasses and serve immediately for best results.

SERVES: **4** | PREPARATION TIME: **10 MINS**

Beetroot, Apple and Ginger Juice

6 small cooked beetroots
4 large Braeburn apples, cored
  and chopped
5 cm (2 in) piece of root ginger, peeled
2 limes, juiced
250 g / 9 oz / 1 cup crushed ice

1. Pass the beetroots, apple and root ginger through a juicer; collect the juice.
2. Combine the juice with the lime juice and crushed ice in a blender.
3. Blitz until smooth before pouring into glasses.
4. Serve immediately, garnishing with a slice of ginger.

Essential Drinks

Carrot Zinger

3 large carrots, sliced
2 medium oranges, quartered
1 knob ginger

1. Process the ingredients through an electronic juicer followed by the pineapple, according to the manufacturer's instructions.
2. Pour into a bottle and shake until thoroughly mixed.

Avocado Calmer

2 ripe avocados, peeled, stoned and cut into chunks
150 g / 5 ½ oz / 1 cup green seedless grapes
1 cucumber, cut into chunks
1 romaine lettuce, cut into chunks
1 lime, halved with 1 slice reserved for the garnish
4 mint leaves

1. Spread the avocado and grapes out on a baking tray and freeze for 3 hours or until solid.
2. Process the cucumber, lettuce and lime through an electronic juicer, according to the manufacturer's instructions.
3. Transfer the juice to a liquidizer and add the mint leaves, the frozen avocado and grapes. Blend until smooth, then pour into a glass and garnish with a slice of lime.

SERVES: **4** | PREPARATION TIME: **5-10 MINS**

Pineapple and Ginger Juice

2 small pineapples, peeled and cored
5 cm (2 in) piece of root ginger, peeled and grated
a small bunch of mint leaves, roughly chopped
a few drops of vanilla extract
350 g / 12 oz / 1 ½ cups crushed iced

1. Roughly chop the pineapple flesh and add to a blender along with the grated ginger, mint leaves and vanilla extract.
2. Blitz until pulpy; add the crushed iced and blitz again until smooth.
3. Pass through a fine sieve into a jug before pouring into glasses and serving.

SERVES: **4** | PREPARATION TIME: **10 MINS**

Melon Juice

2 charentais melons
a pinch of salt
250 g / 9 oz / 1 cup crushed ice

1. Quarter the melons and discard the seeds before roughly chopping the flesh.
2. Sprinkle a pinch of salt over the flesh before blitzing in a blender until smooth; pass through a sieve back into the blender.
3. Add the crushed ice and blitz again until smooth.
4. Pass through a fine sieve into glasses before serving.

SERVES: **2** | PREPARATION TIME: **5 MINS**

Cranberry and Apple Juice

400 g / 14 oz / 4 cups cranberries
2 red apples, quartered
3 oranges, quartered
50 ml / 1 ¾ fl. oz / ¼ cup sugar
  (simple) syrup

1. Process the cranberries, apple and orange through an electronic juicer, according to the manufacturer's instructions.
2. Pour the juice into a jug and stir in sugar syrup to taste.
3. Chill in the fridge until you're ready to serve.

Lime and
Strawberry Juice

250 g / 9 oz / 1 ⅔ cups strawberries
2 tbsp mint, chopped, plus a few sprigs
2 limes, halved
6 ice cubes

1. Slice one of the strawberries. Use one slice to garnish the glass and put
   the other slices inside with the mint sprigs, two slices of lime and the
   ice cubes.
2. Process the rest of the strawberries, chopped mint and lime through an
   electronic juicer, according to the manufacturer's instructions.
3. Pour the juice into the glass and serve immediately.

Green Goodness
Juice

2 Granny Smith apples, quartered
2 kiwi fruit, halved
2 large cabbage leaves, rolled up tightly
1 lime, one slice reserved and the
  rest quartered
1 ripe avocado, peeled and stoned

1. Process the apple, kiwi, cabbage and lime through an electronic juicer,
   according to the manufacturer's instructions.
2. Transfer the juice to a liquidizer, add the avocado and blend until smooth.
3. Pour the juice into a glass and serve garnished with the reserved lime slice.

Watermelon Dill Juice

250 g / 9 oz / 1 cup crushed ice
250 ml / 9 fl. oz / 1 cup cold water
½ lime, juiced
½ watermelon, flesh cubed
2 tbsp agave nectar
a small bunch of dill, chopped

1. Combine the ice, water, lime juice and watermelon in a blender.
2. Blitz until smooth before adding the agave nectar and two tablespoons of chopped dill.
3. Blitz again before passing through a sieve into a jug.
4. Garnish with more dill before serving.

Carrot and Orange Juice

3 carrots
1 orange, quartered

1. Process the carrots and orange through an electronic juicer, according to the manufacturer's instructions.
2. Pour the juice into a bottle and chill until ready to serve.

Apple Juice with Frozen Berries

4 apples, quartered
450 g / 1 lb / 3 cups frozen
  mixed berries
2 frozen raspberries, to garnish

1. Process the apples through an electronic juicer, according to the manufacturer's instructions.
2. Transfer the juice to a liquidizer and add the frozen berries. Blend until smooth, then pour into two glasses.
3. Garnish each one with a frozen raspberry and serve immediately.

SERVES: **1** | PREPARATION TIME: **4 MINS**

Fresh Grape Juice

350 g / 12 ½ oz / 4 cups red grapes
2 ice cubes

1. Slice one of the grapes in half and use to garnish a tumbler.
2. Process the grapes through an electronic juicer, according to the manufacturer's instructions.
3. Pour the juice into the glass and add a couple of ice cubes.

SERVES: **2** | PREPARATION TIME: **5 MINS**

Quick Mint Limeade

5 limes, halved
25 g / 1 oz / 1 cup mint leaves
50 ml / 1 ¾ oz / ¼ cup sugar (simple) syrup
2 handfuls ice cubes
300 ml / 10 ½ fl. oz / 1 ¼ cup sparkling water

1. Slice one of the lime halves and divide between two glasses with a few of the mint leaves and the ice.
2. Process the rest of the limes and mint through an electronic juicer and pour over the ice.
3. Top up with sparkling water and stir well before serving.

Beetroot and Raspberry Juice

1 red apple, quartered
2 beetroot, quartered
150 g / 5 ½ oz / 1 cup raspberries

1. Process the ingredients through an electronic juicer, according to the manufacturer's instructions.
2. Pour the juice into a jar, tightly screw on the lid and refrigerate until ready to serve.
3. Shake well before drinking.

Spinach and Avocado Smoothie

4 stalks celery
2 large handfuls spinach leaves
1 cucumber
2 ripe avocados, peeled and stoned

1. Process the celery, spinach and cucumber through an electronic juicer, according to the manufacturer's instructions.
2. Transfer the juice to a liquidizer, add the avocados and blend until smooth.
3. Pour the mixture into two glasses and serve garnished with a spinach leaf or celery leaf.

Watermelon and Lime Juice

6 limes
½ watermelon, flesh cubed
2 tbsp agave nectar
600 g / 1 lb 5 oz / 2 ½ cups crushed ice

1. Halve 4 of the limes and juice them into a blender.
2. Add the watermelon flesh, agave nectar and half of the crushed ice; blitz until smooth before passing through a sieve into a jug.
3. Slice the remaining limes and arrange them in ice-filled glasses.
4. Pour over the juice and serve immediately for best results.

Summer Fruits and Orange Smoothie

6 oranges, segmented
110 g / 4 oz / 1 cup redcurrants
100 g / 3 ½ oz / ⅔ cup raspberries
110 g / 4 oz / ½ cup vanilla yogurt
250 g / 9 oz / 1 cup crushed ice

1. Blitz together the orange segments, redcurrants and raspberries in a blender; pass through a fine sieve back into the blender.
2. Add the yogurt and crushed ice; blitz again until smooth.
3. Pour into glasses and serve immediately for best results.

SERVES: **2** | PREPARATION TIME: **5 MINS**

Fennel, Lime and Lemon Juice

1 lemon, halved
2 limes, halved
1 bulb fennel, quartered
2 tbsp sugar (simple) syrup
1 handful ice cubes
chilled water to dilute

1. Cut a couple of slices from one of the lemon and lime halves and set aside.
2. Process the fennel and the rest of the lemon and limes through an electronic juicer.
3. Fill a glass with ice and add the reserved lemon and lime slices. Pour over the juice and stir in the sugar syrup.
4. Dilute with chilled water to taste then serve immediately.

Mango Juice

2 ripe mangoes, pitted
1 lime, juiced
1 tsbp agave nectar
250 g / 9 oz / 1 cup crushed ice

1. Roughly chop the mango flesh before adding to a blender along with the lime juice, agave nectar and crushed ice.
2. Blitz until smooth before passing through a sieve into glasses.
3. Serve immediately for best results.

SERVES: **4** | PREPARATION TIME: **10 MINS**

Watermelon Juice

1 large watermelon, deseeded and diced
½ lime, juiced
250 g / 9 oz / 1 cup crushed ice
a pinch of salt

1. Combine the watermelon and lime juice in a blender; blitz until smooth, working batches if necessary.
2. Pass the juice through a sieve and back into the blender.
3. Add the ice and a pinch of salt before blitzing again until smooth and frothy.
4. Pour into glasses and serve immediately for best results.

Index